CW01429176

What If?

Volume 3

What If? Volume 3
by Brian Brooks

Copyright ©2015 Brian Brooks.
All rights reserved.

Edited by Emily Wick

ISBN-13: 978-1512255775
ISBN-10: 1512255777

Published by
Smokey's TANGLE
4709 Telegraph Ave
Oakland, California 94609
www.smokeystangle.com

First printing: May 2015
ST016

What If?
Volume 3

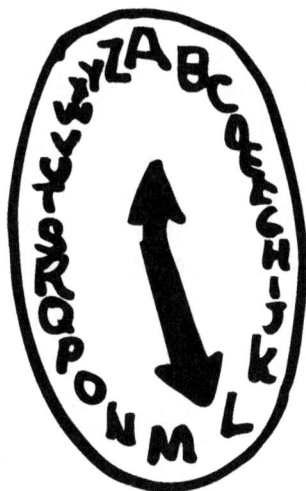

by Brian Brooks

Smokey's TANGLE
Oakland

What if we could do math with emoticons?

What if we bred horses
for more riders?

What if Earth started spinning faster and everyone had to run in place just to stand still?

What if we used bits
of string and thread
as our currency?

What if the moon
had a giant stuffed
animal?

What if people used
human glue instead of
marriage counselors?

What if humans never
discovered spooning?

What if the size of our
telephones had kept pace
with the size of our
televisions?

What if there was
only one thought?

What if soda manufacturers started selling us nothing?

What if mirrors reflected
the exact opposite of what
was and sometimes that was
so distrurbing you couldn't
look away?

What if every screw head
was unique and needed
its own individualized
screwdriver?

What if ants thought
shoes were gods?

What if walls were made
out of opaque glass?

What if they introduced
an ultimate letter which
replaced all other letters
and became the only
letter we ever needed?

What if they kept intro-
ducing new letters to our
alphabet but didn't tell
us how to use them?

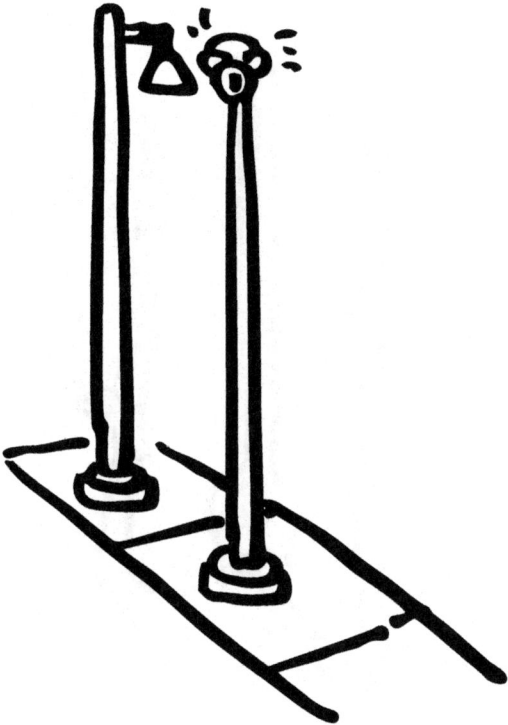

What if in addition to
street lights we had street
alarm clocks?

What if every time you ever spoke, someone on the other side of the world mimicked you like a puppet?

What if everyone in Manhattan
looked at your Facebook page
all day long because it was
their job?

What if photographs showed
the future and once you
saw your photograph you
knew what you had to do?

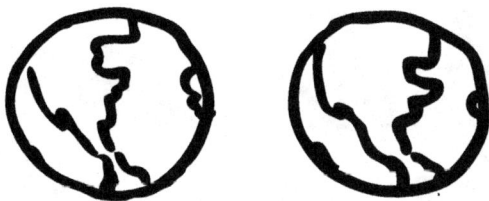

What if there was another
Earth that was identical
except for six differences
that gods tried to find
when they were bored?

What if no two paper clips were alike?

What if instead of locks
we placed additional desir-
able items around the
things we wanted to keep?

What if time was measured
in songs and you had to
carry around a boom box
if you had an appointment?

What if some pigeons
were superheroes?

What if there was a
no-thrill shelter for
unwanted novelty
invisible-dog-on-a-leashes?

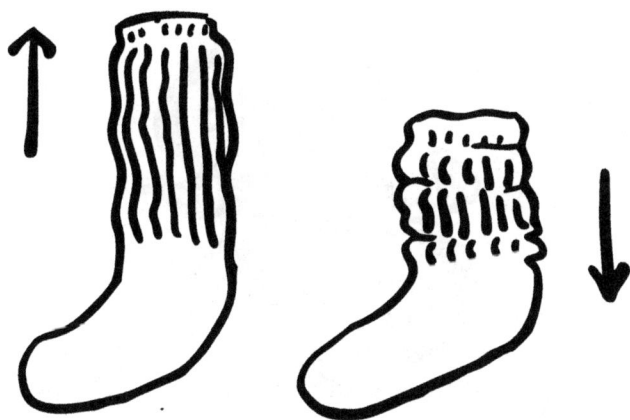

What if every time you
pulled up your socks. . .
someone's socks on the
other side of the world
were pulled down?

What if bicycles
learned how to ride
people, and once they
learned, they never
forgot?

What if there was only
one comic ever made but
it was so funny that it
was all we ever needed?

What if dinosaurs made
it off the planet?

What if Scrabble® for
ducks contained mostly
Qs and Us?

What if people
walked sideways?

What if pizza slices
were shaped like
Christmas trees?

What if the sun let out an unmistakable "Later Dudes" every time it set over the ocean, and only surfers could hear it?

What if our jobs could
all be conducted via
drive-thru?

What if we kept our
telephones out front
by the mailbox?

What if dogs, cats, and
squirrels roamed around
on Big Wheels?

What if humans were un-
wittingly entering into
unknown agreements with
every shake of a dog's paw?

What if trees kept people
on treadmills like we keep
houseplants?

What if packages were
delivered by fancy
waiters?

What if humming was
the greatest offense?

What if our fingers
independently snapped
when our hands were
happy?

What if wastepaper
baskets grew in size
until they eventually
became dumpsters?

What if bicycles
learned how to
walk upright?

What if clouds were
just placeholders for
something God hadn't
invented yet?

What if a Rubik's Cube
solved all of the
world's problems?

What if every worm
that ever came across a
lost cell phone ordered
a pizza with dirt and
leaves as toppings?

What if all shadows were
just groups of bugs who
were afraid of the sun?

What if instead of string
we used ants holding hands?

What if ghosts were
afraid of hooks and
nails?

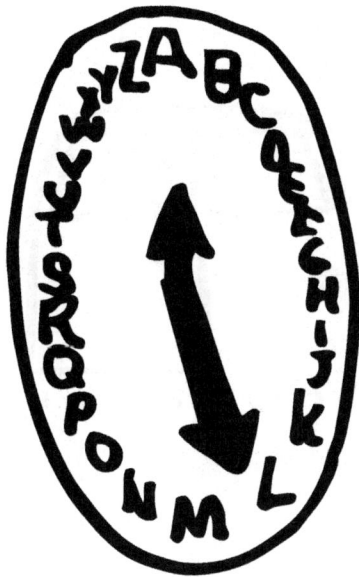

What if we told time with
letters instead of numbers?

What if cars were bolted
to the ground and were
where you went when you
didn't want to go anywhere?

What if some people could see the future but could only use dance to describe what they saw?

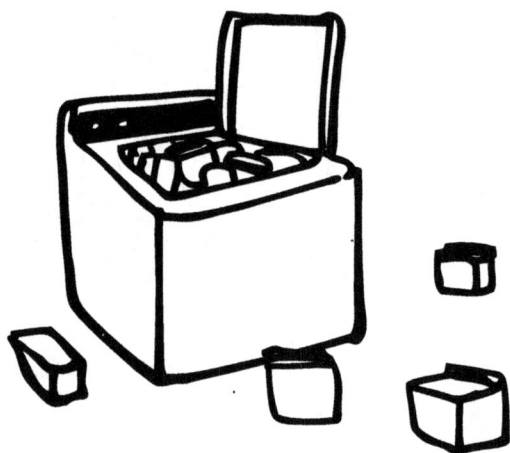

What if washing machines
had to be washed in giant
washing machines?

What if every stickman
ever drawn came to life?

What if you could purchase success but it was so expensive that only rich people bought it?

What if fire hydrants were
old robots that had to pee
so badly that they couldn't
take another step?

What if t-shirts were made with armholes for limbs our species hadn't developed yet?

What if bank tellers
had to tell you a story
and sometimes it took a
very long time?

What if cows were used as
cowbell holders and were
a part of every drum kit?

What if snakes ate
bunnies but stopped
at their heads and then
slithered around scaring
the other animals?

What if blank paper
was sold as crumpled-
up balls?

What if gift wrap was
applied as a liquid?

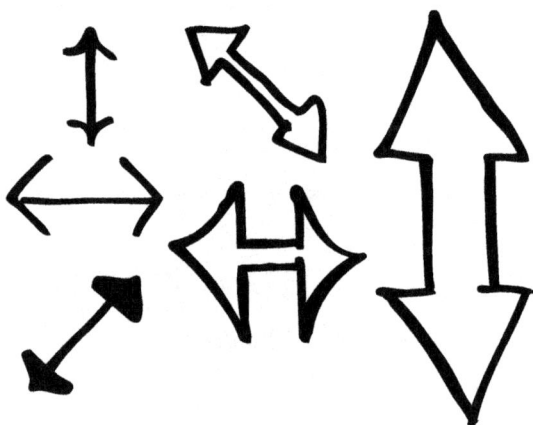

What if the other ends of
arrows were granted equal
rights?

What if soccer balls
filed a class action
lawsuit against soccer
players?

What if chairs moved
and put their tables
up for sale?

What if instead of sirens
emergency vehicles used
strong scents?

What if you could lay
down in some restaurants
and the servers would
spoon you?

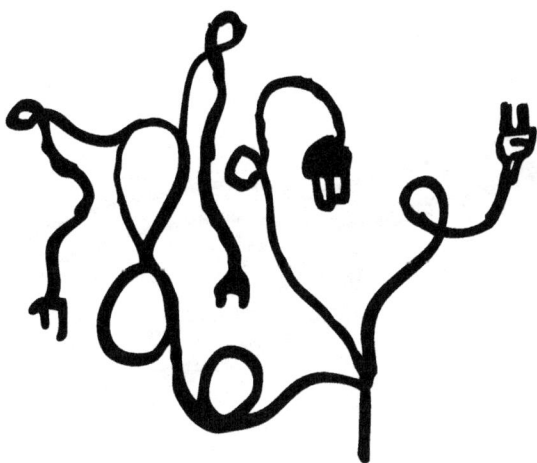

What if extention cord
designers were more
creative?

What if there were
specially shaped plates
for serving cat?

What if snakes had to stay
in the "S" shape?

What if there was a
larvae-type creature
at the center of Earth
who was sort of in
charge of everything?

What if every fossil is
actually part of one giant
dinosaur?

What if each tree produced
only one giant fruit?

What if birthday candles
required being lit by
the Eternal Birthday
Flame?

What if spools had
never been invented?

What if shot glasses were
super thin and really tall?

What if instead of
jobs, we all had to
have Bobs?

What if humans
evolved to have rear-
view mirrors?

What if helmets were
built into motorcycles?

What if museums
were showcases for frames,
and the art was just a
placeholder?

What if we redrew state
borders to be stars and
stripes?

What if CD booklets were
humankind's crowning
achievement?

What if the bank teller
had to tell you specifically
what to buy with which
dollar?

What if rich people
bought diamonds by
the cereal box full?

What if humans had
secret compartments
like Swiss Army knives?

What if we drew our
calendars differently?

What if dummers drummed
with rocks instead of
sticks?

What if when one
interviewer interviewed
another interviewer,
they both disappeared?

What if every single person
needed a pair of tickets?

What if spills were sold
separately?

What if some people
got ingrown baseball
cap bills?

What if pizzas were delivered by tossing them like a Frisbee and breadsticks like boomerangs?

What if milkshakes had to be jogged to your table by top-less lactating women with large breasts?

What if soft blankets
had never been invented?

What if humans were so
careful that not a single
light switch plate or
electric socket cover had
ever even been touched
by a single drop of paint?

What if smart phones
had their own cell
phones?

What if Ben & Jerry's
ice cream had ponytails?

What if, instead of delivery,
UPS and FED-EX kidnapped
recipients and brought them
to their packages?

What if paper was black
and ink was white?

What if gum was sold
in wad form?

What if bunny ears
grew on bunny tails?

What if you saw a wild
heard of clawfoot tubs?

What if robots kept
tuna cans in aquariums
as pets?

What if snow angels
came to life?

What if some dust bunnies
were world famous?

What if there were
professional litterbugs
who walked around all
day littering?

What if you found every
key that had ever been
lost?

What if we called muscles
"dudes" and said of large-
muscled men that they had
"big dudies"?

63241832
45138743
6457896
43214873
87324329
532814 75°

What if an absurdly long
number was needed to say
what the tempertature was
on a nice day?

What if we had to write
the names of our bags and
affix them to ourselves
when we traveled?

STOP DUSTING

What if dust spelled
messages to us when
it settled?

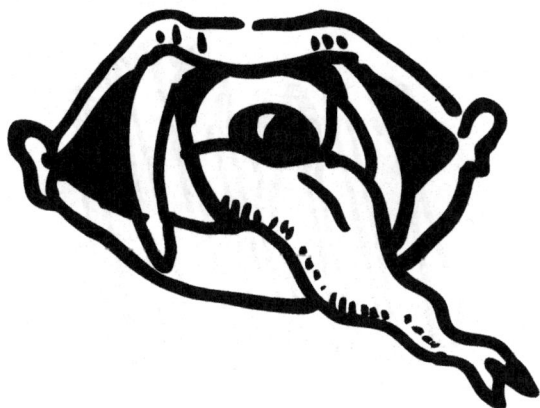

What if we had one
single orifice where
we received all of
our sensory input?

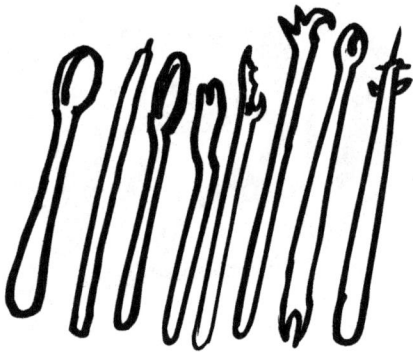

What if we needed a specially-tailored utensil for each bite?

What if you had to take
everything you wanted to keep
out of your house once a week
and the garbage people came
inside and took the rest?

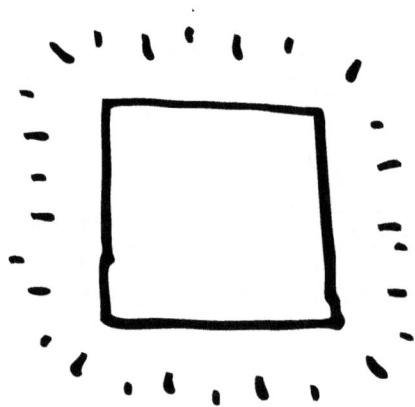

What if the sun
was square?

What if you had to hold
all of your questions
until the end of your life?

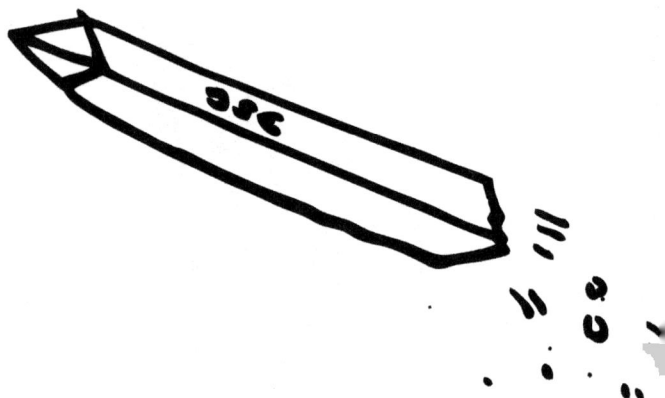

What if our country's last line of defense was using the Washington Monument as a rocket, piloted by the President?

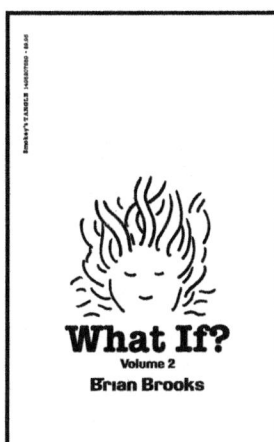

ALSO AVAILABLE

What If?
Volumes 1 & 2

What If? Volume 1
ST003

What If? Volume 2
ST011

ORDER ONE OR TWO TODAY!

Smokey's TANGLE
www.smokeystangle.com

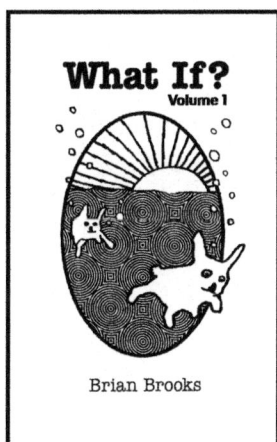

Printed in Dunstable, United Kingdom

65003634R00078